WELCOME
TO
Color Me Botanicals II
An Adult Coloring Book

Please visit our website for more information on new designs,
books and prints at
www.BotanicalArtDesigns.com

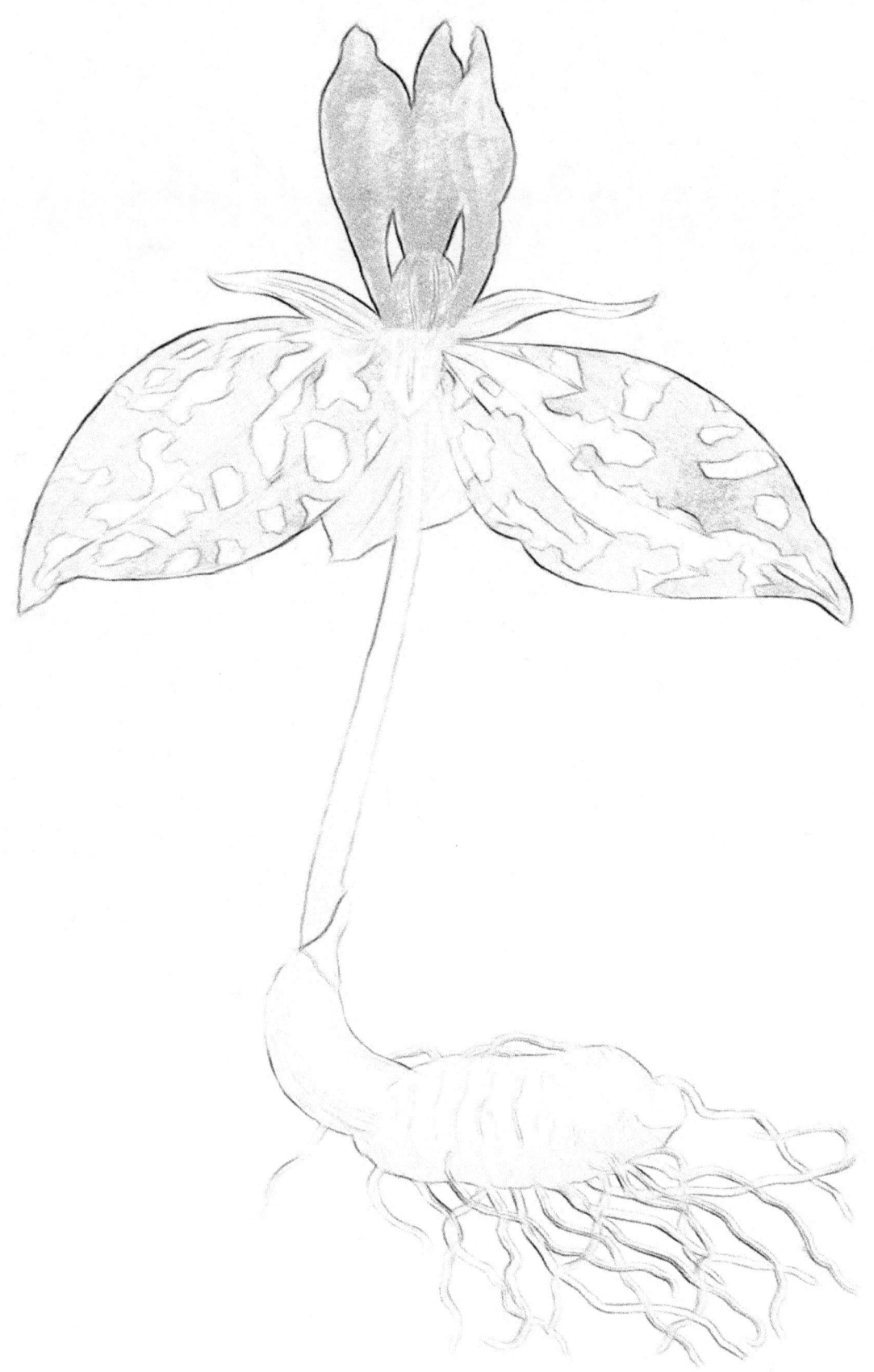

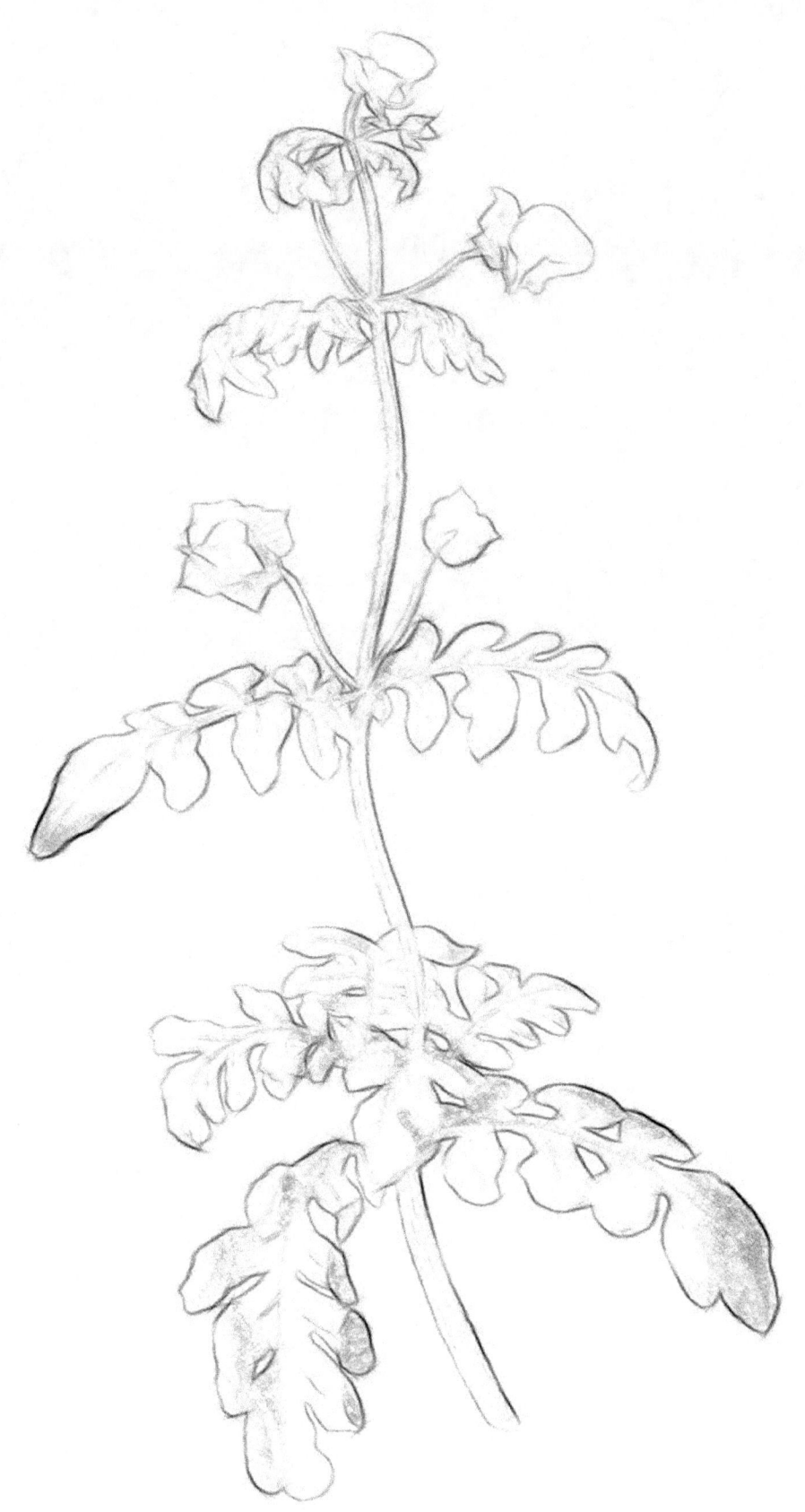

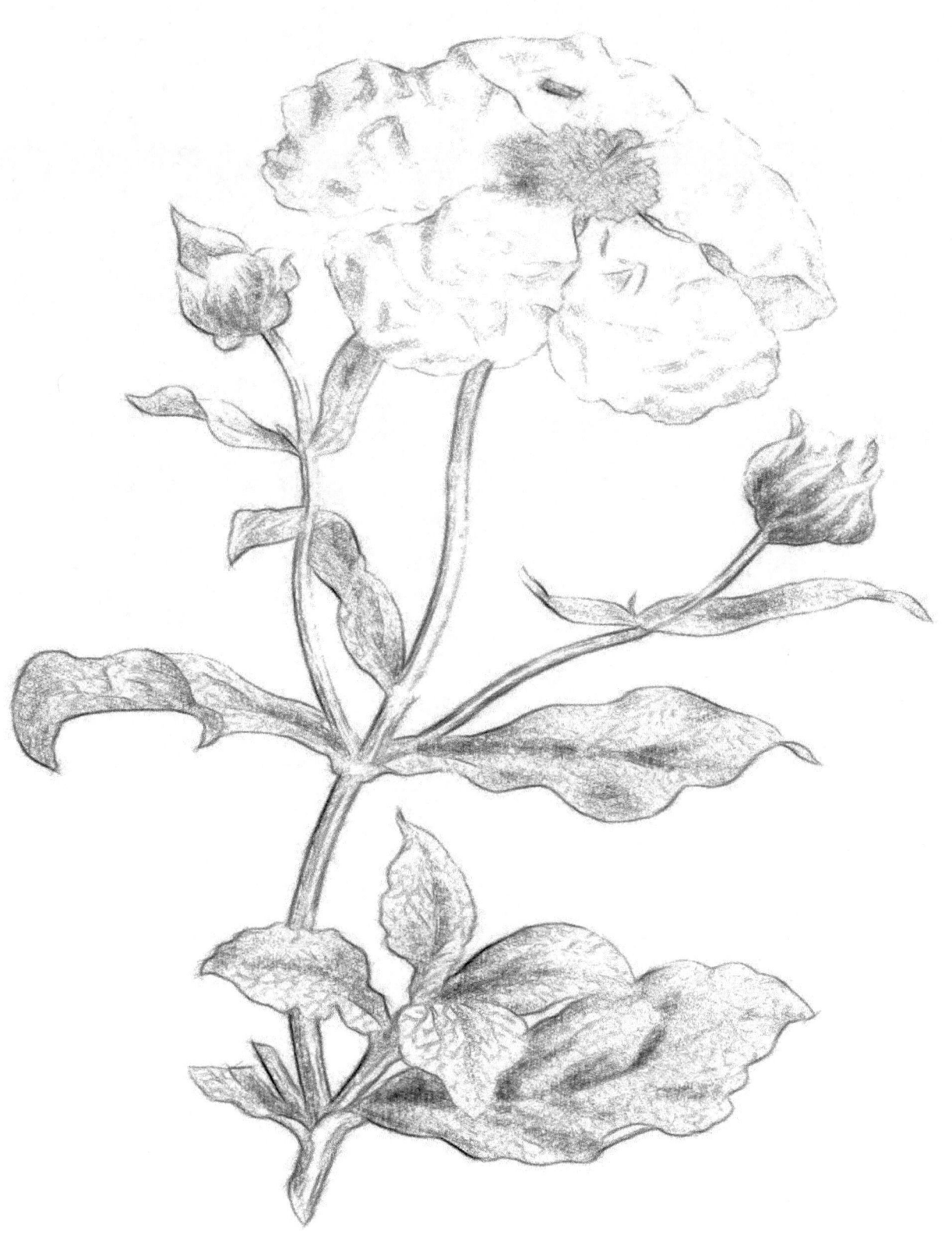

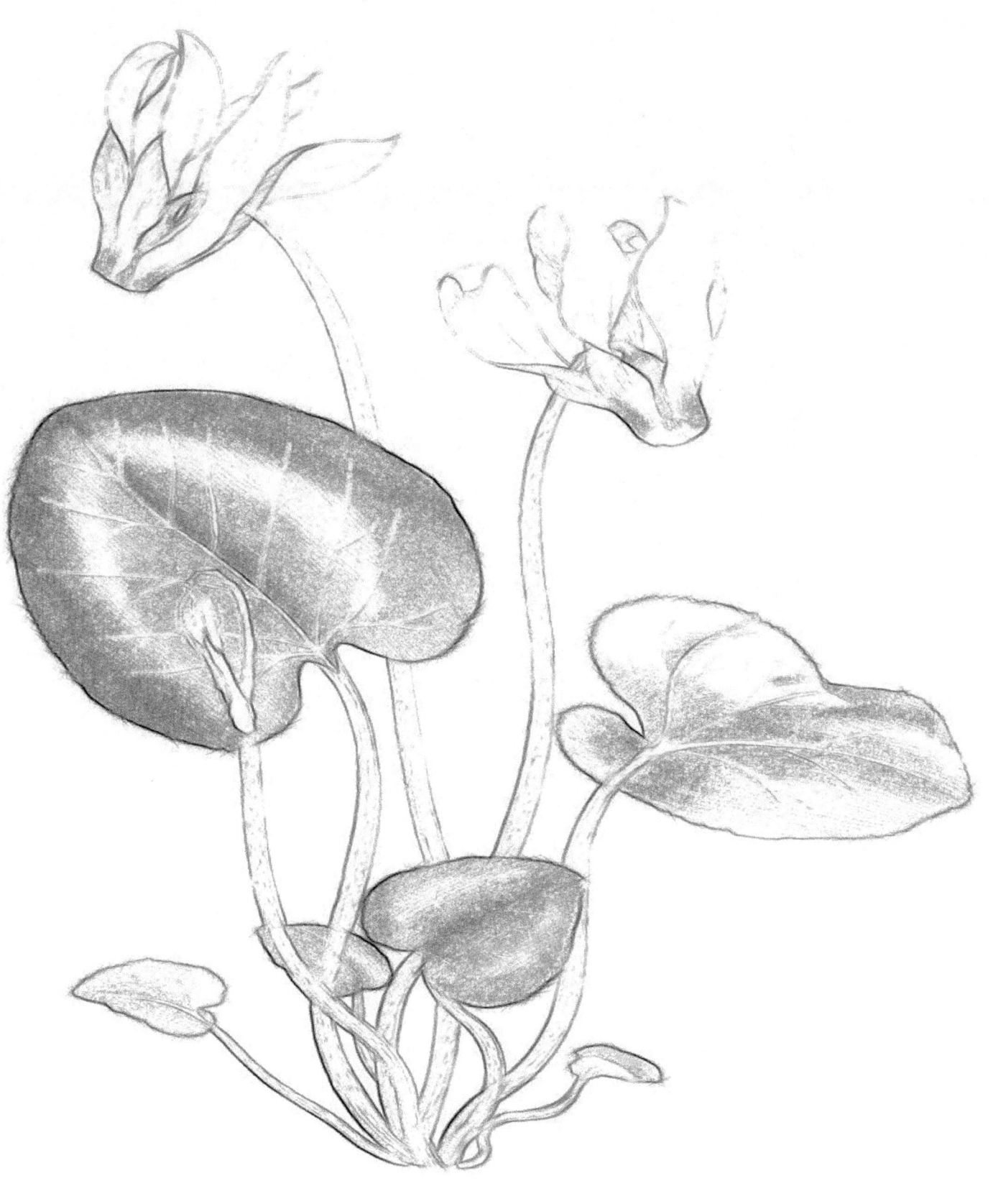

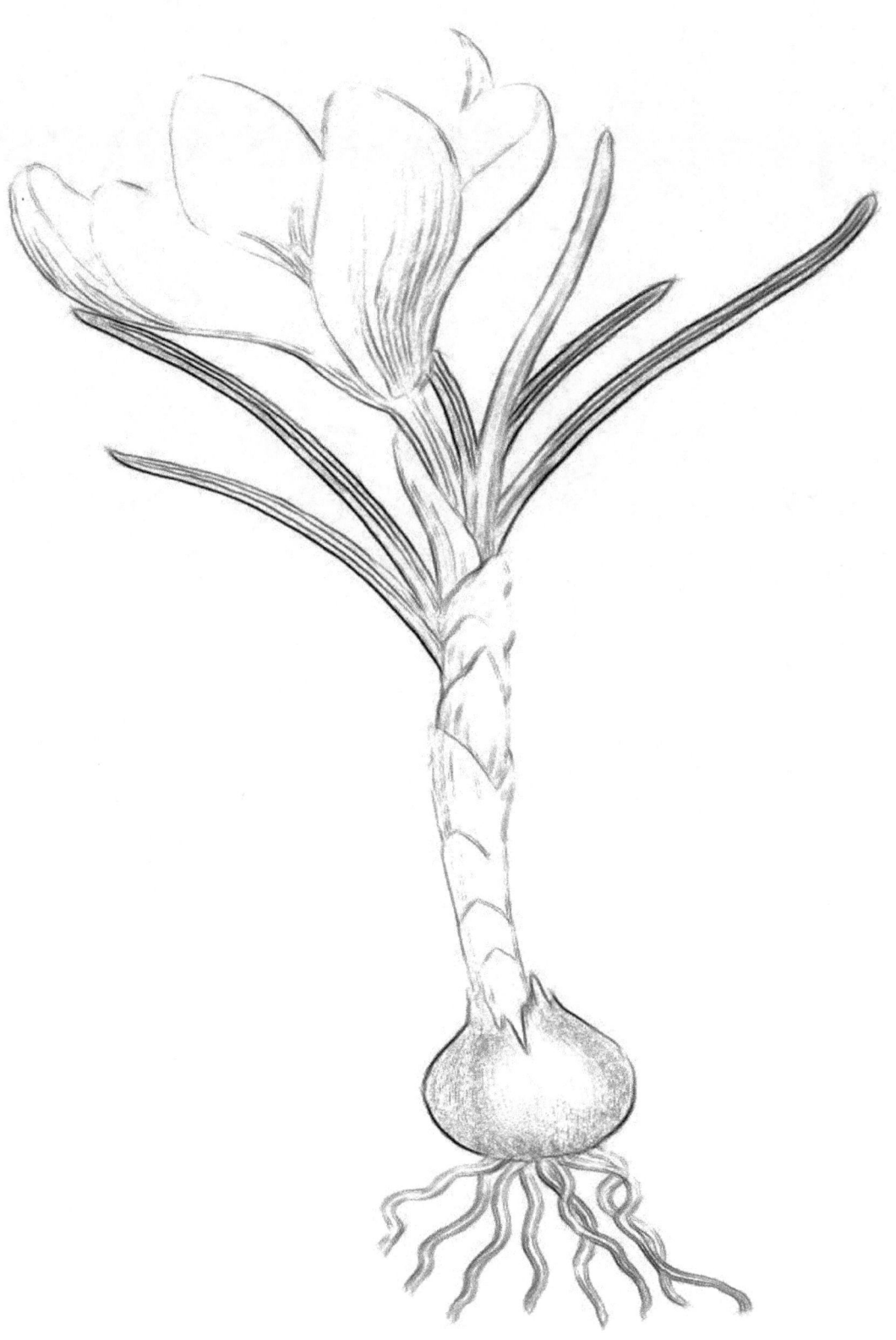

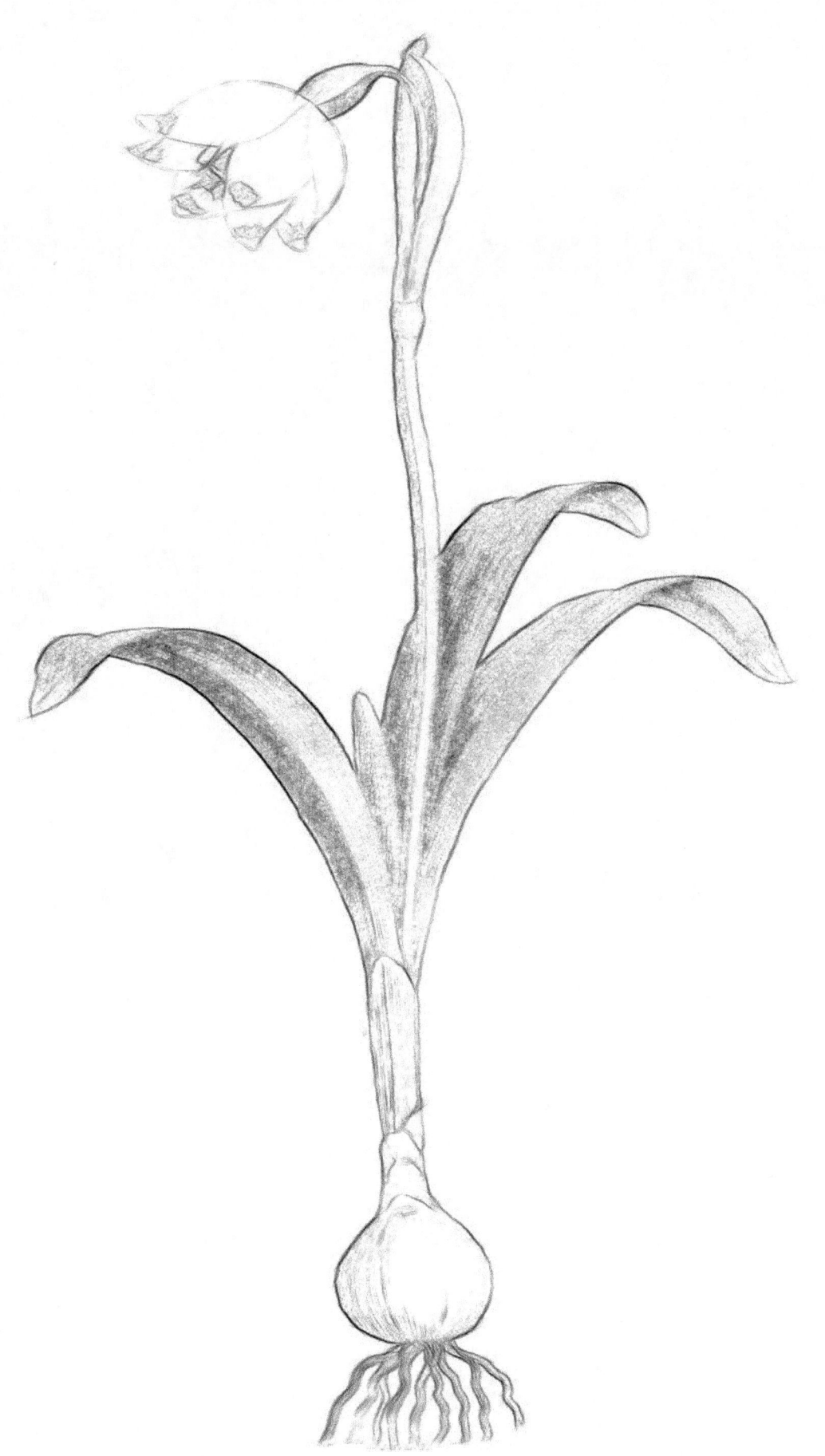

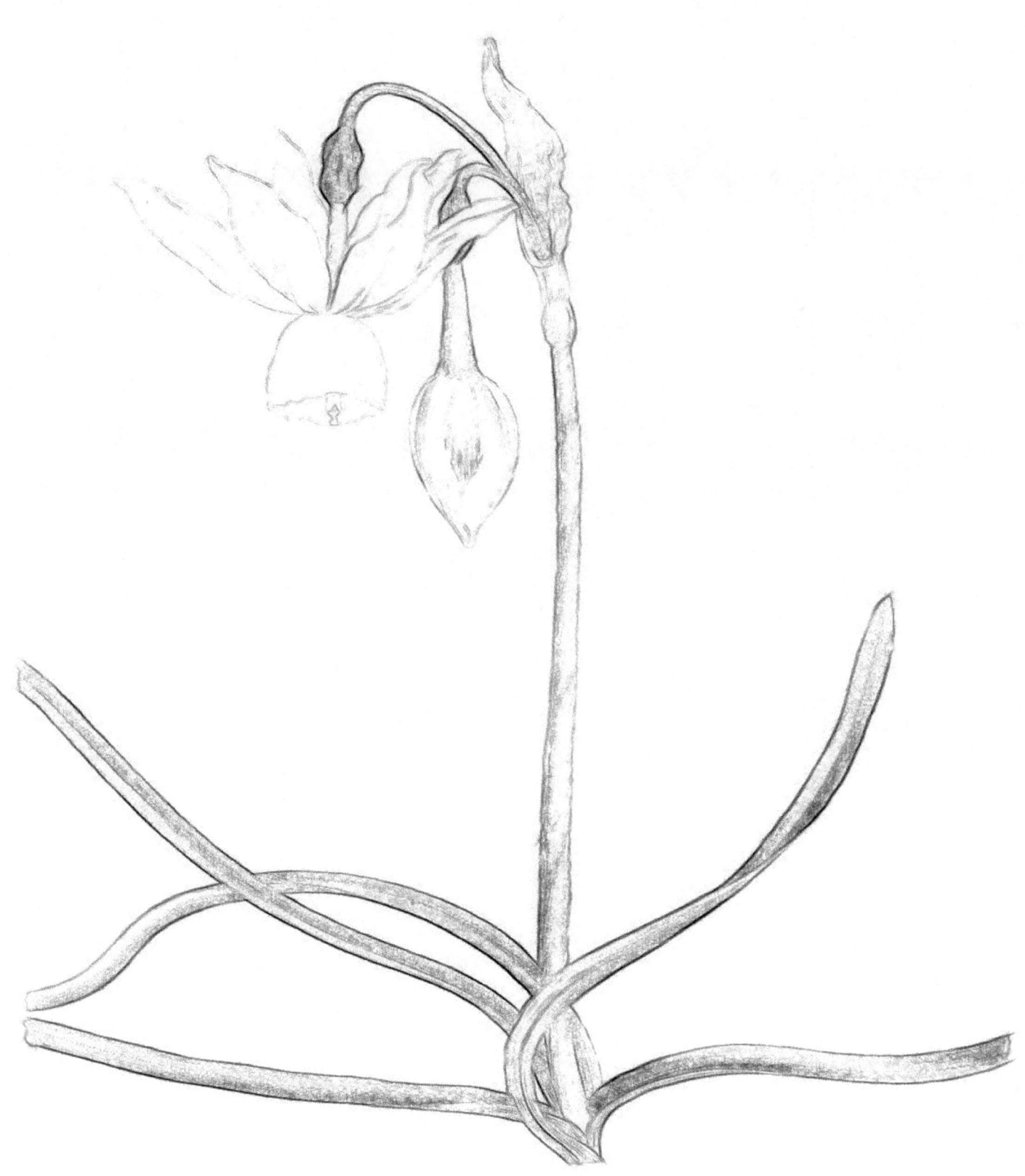

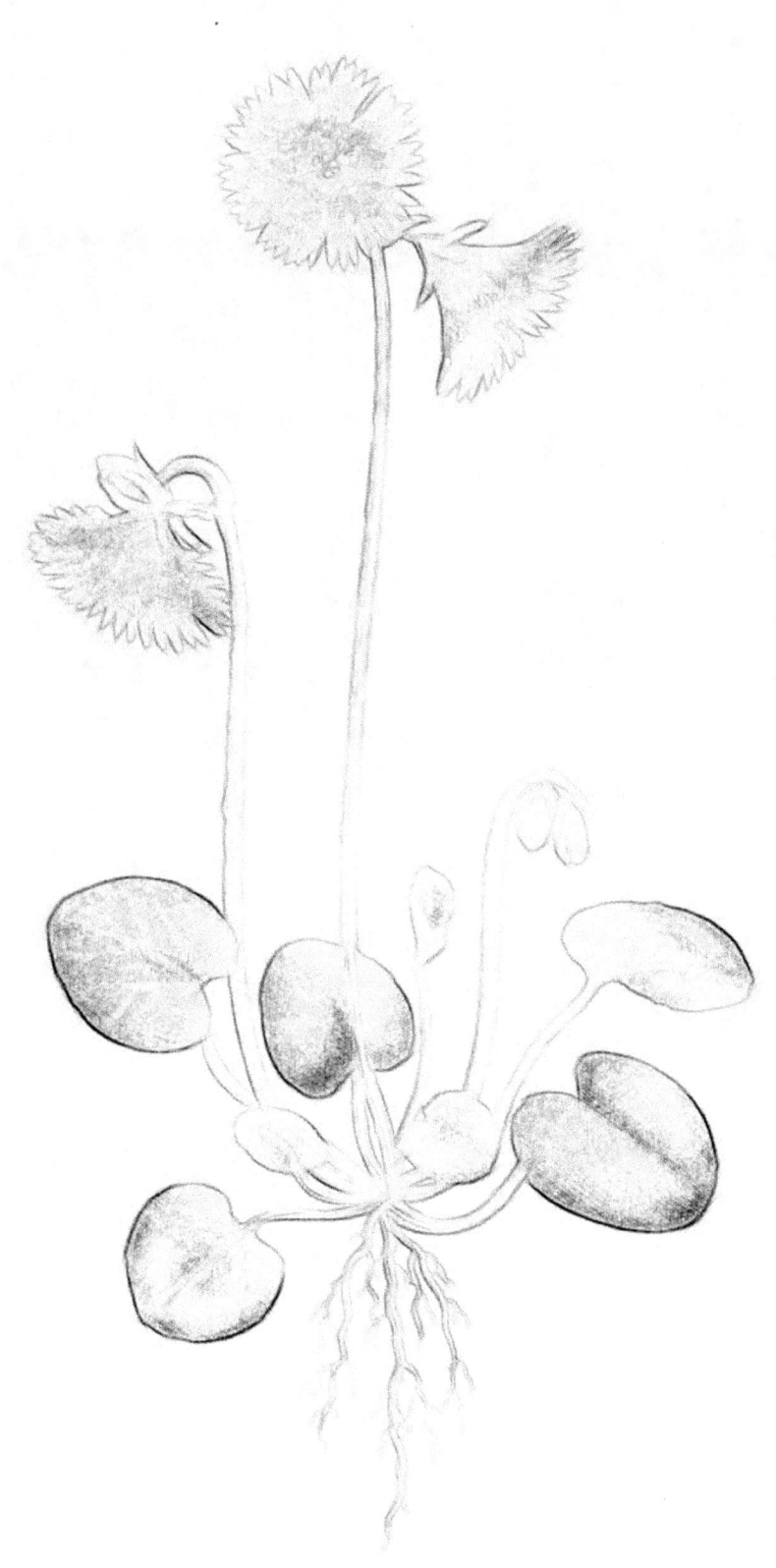

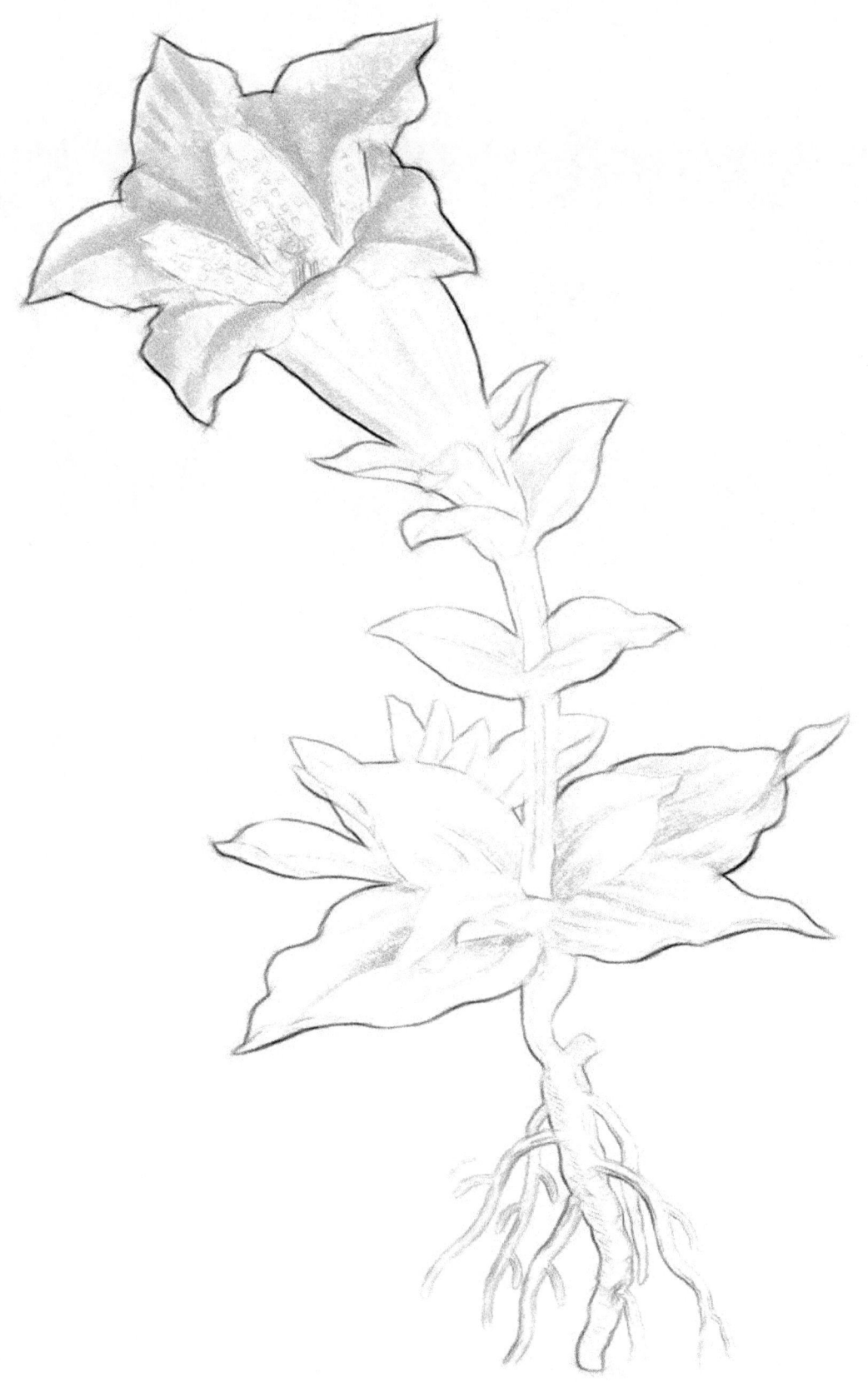

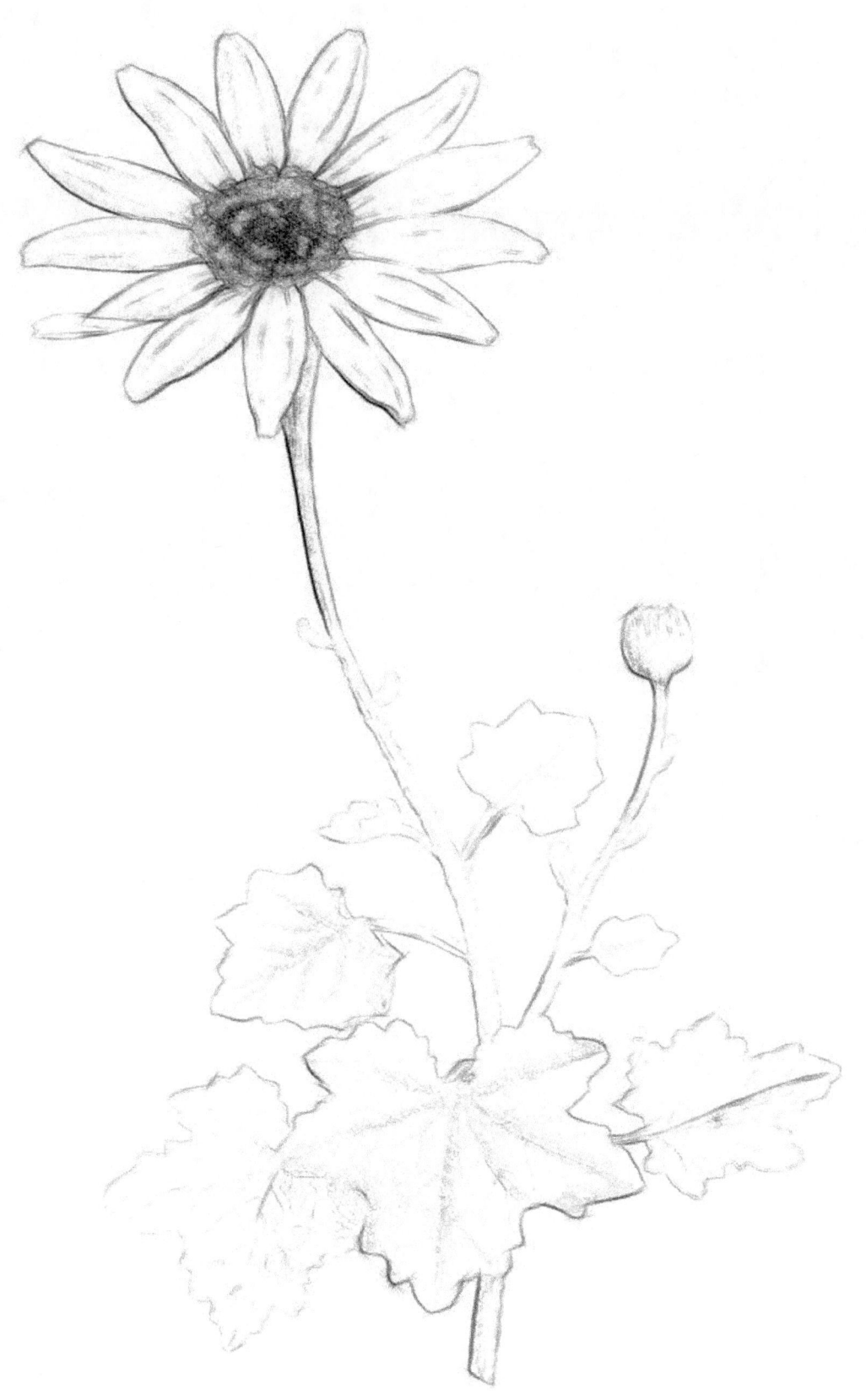

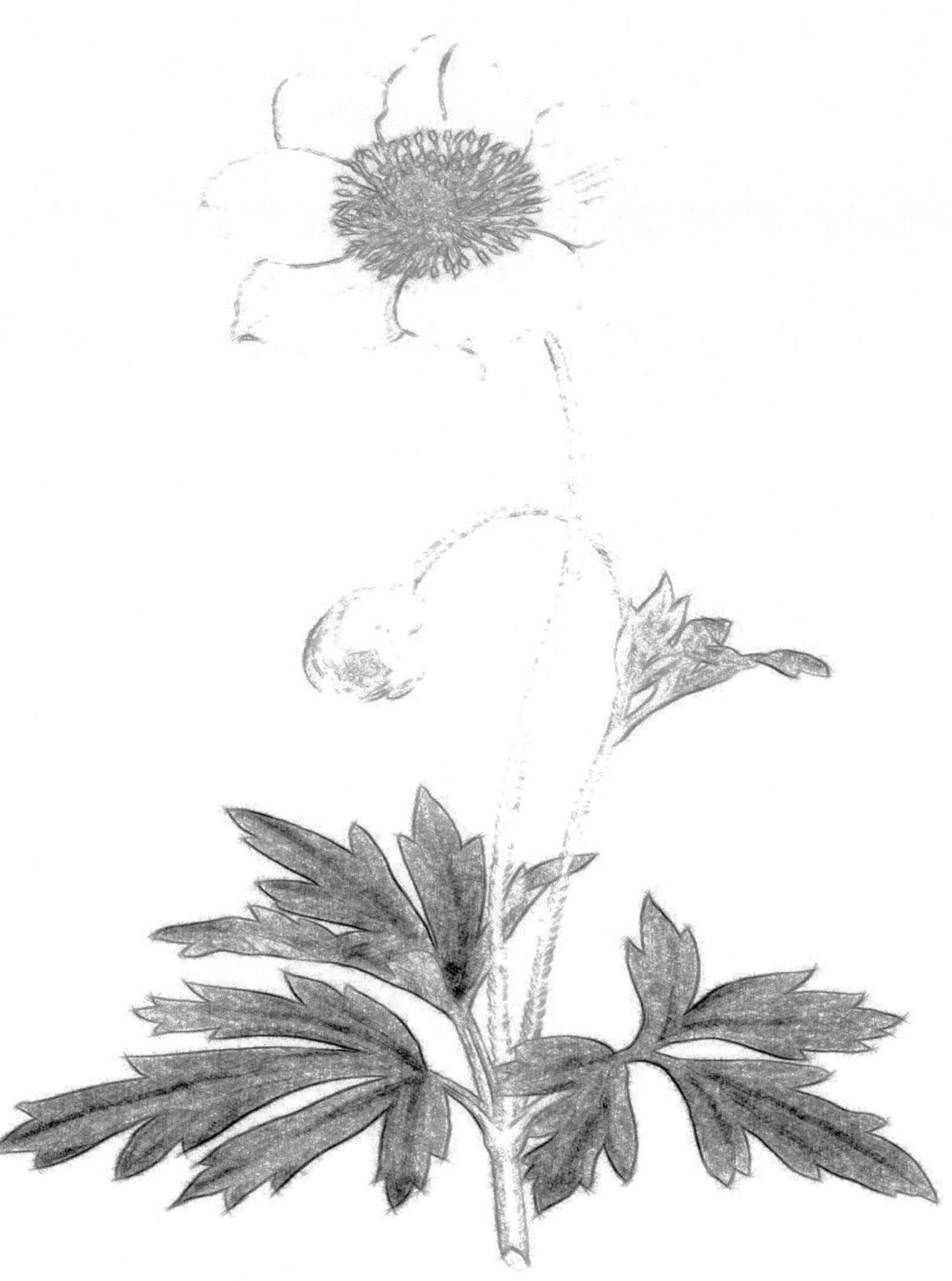

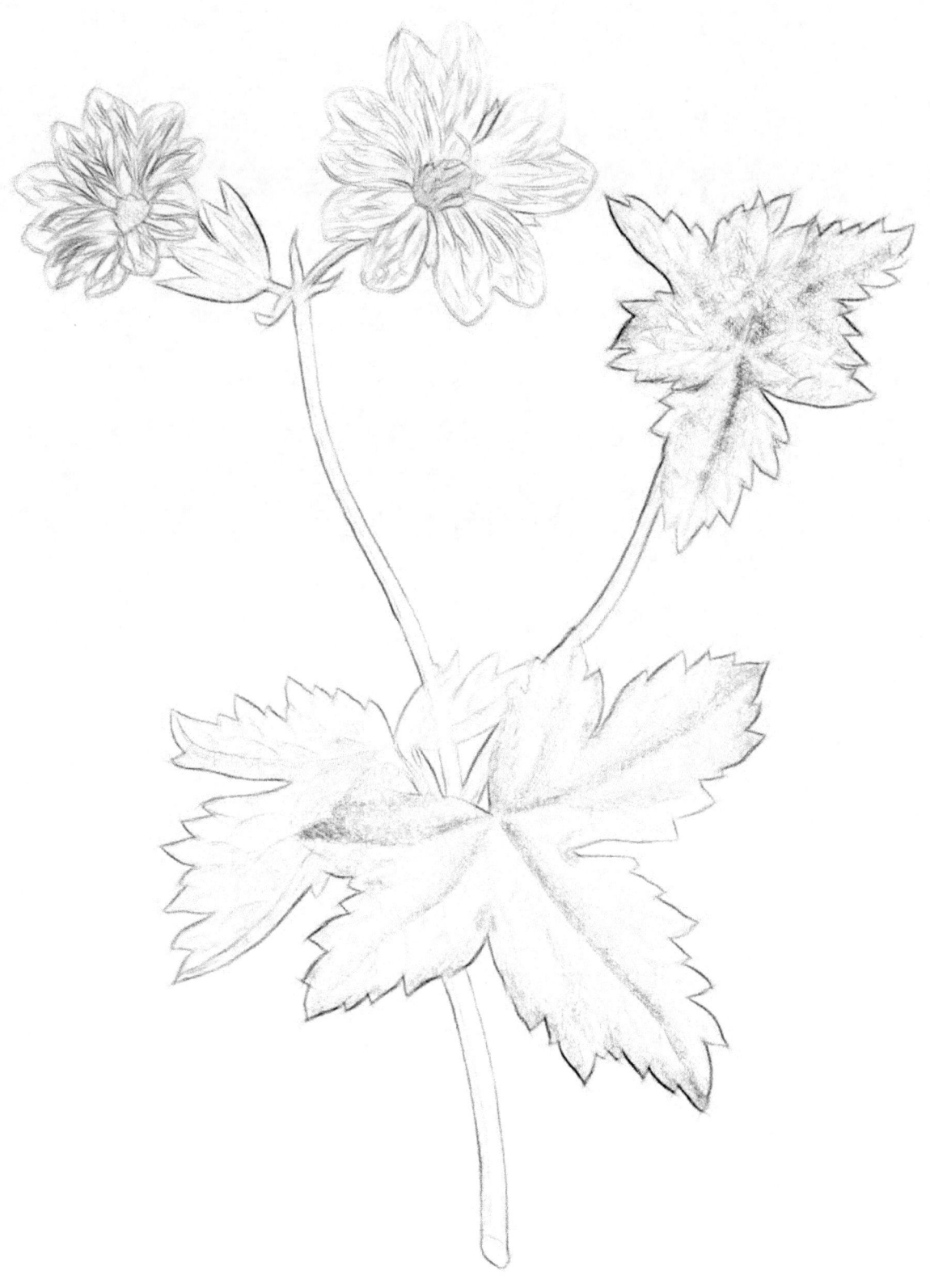

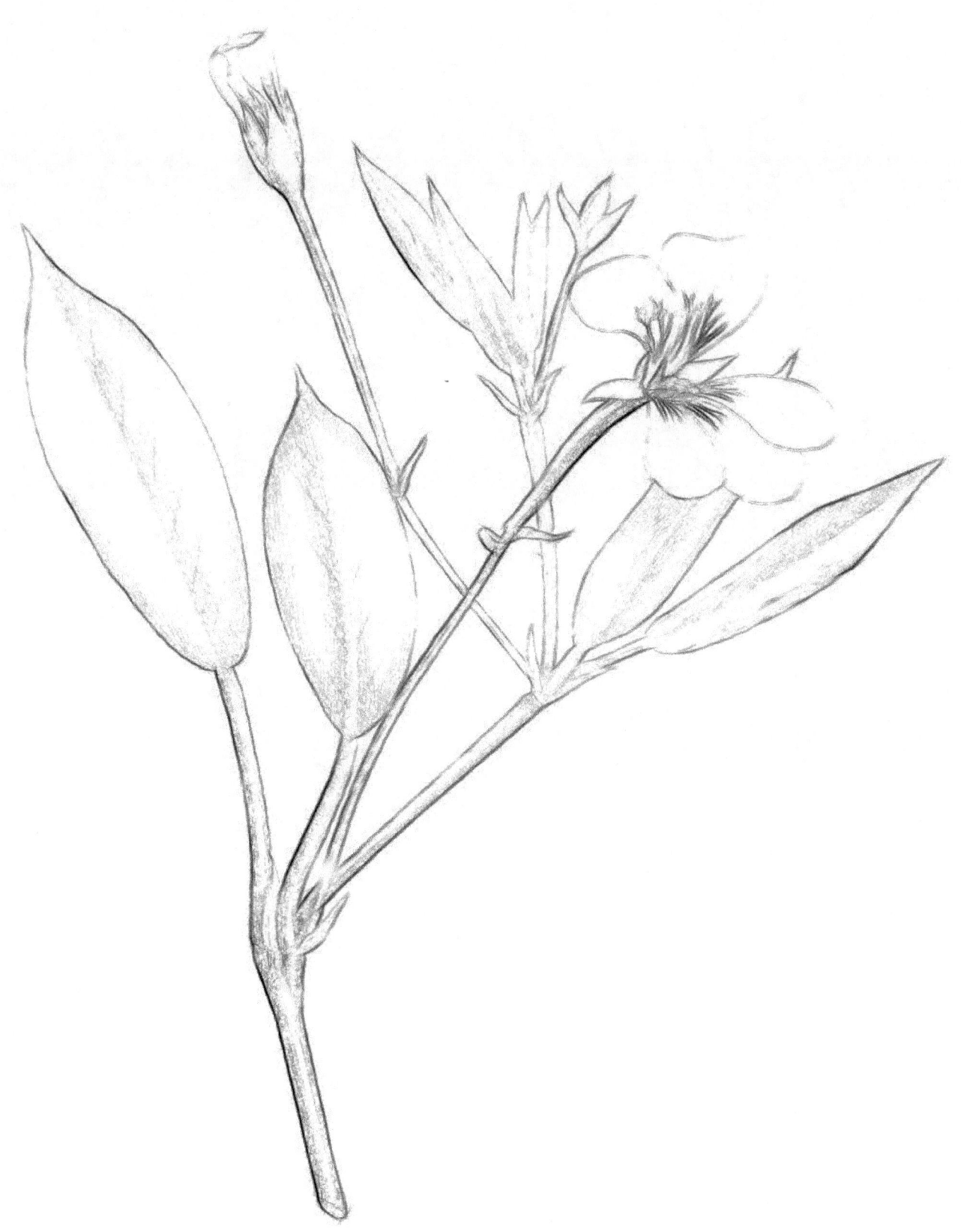

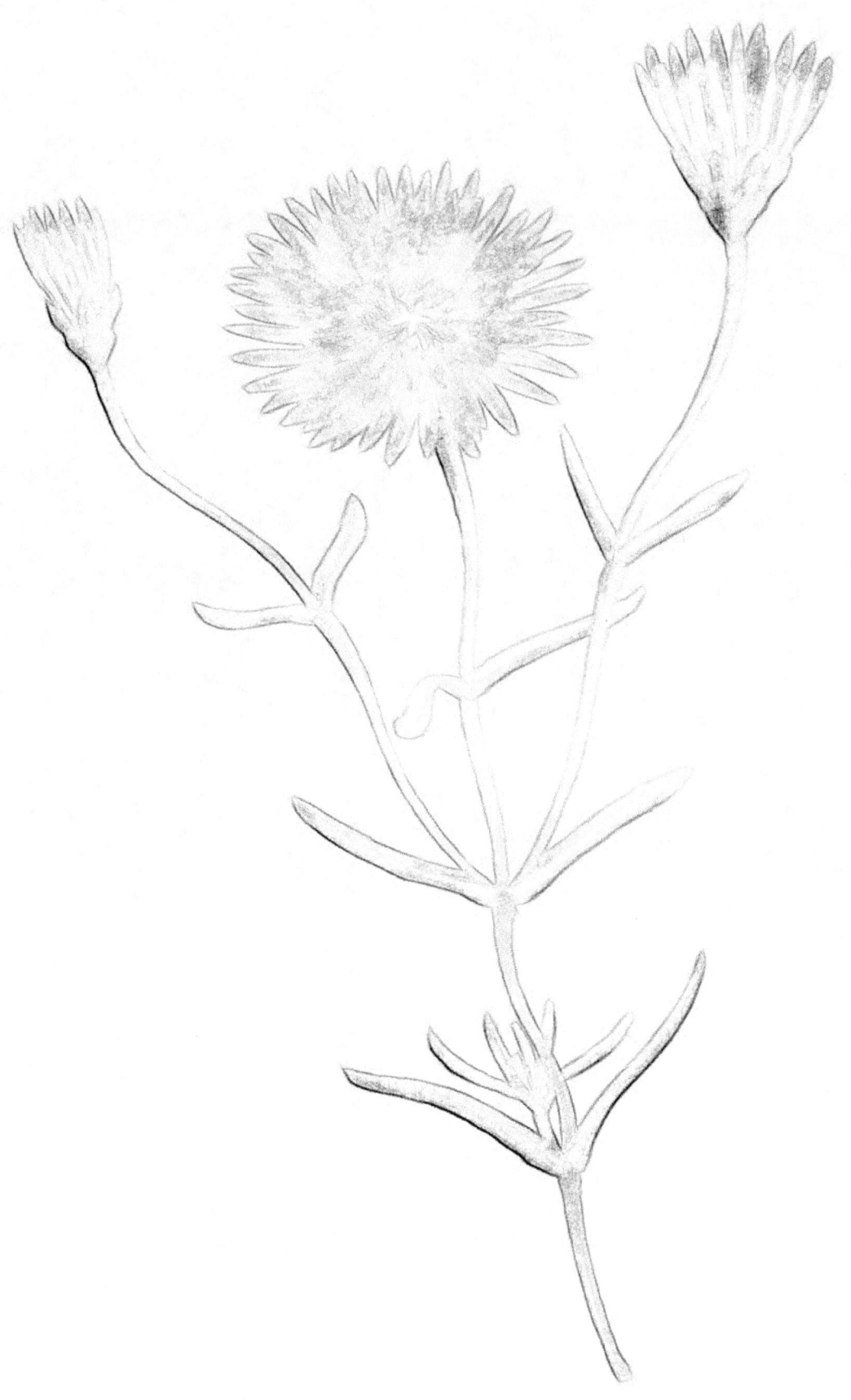

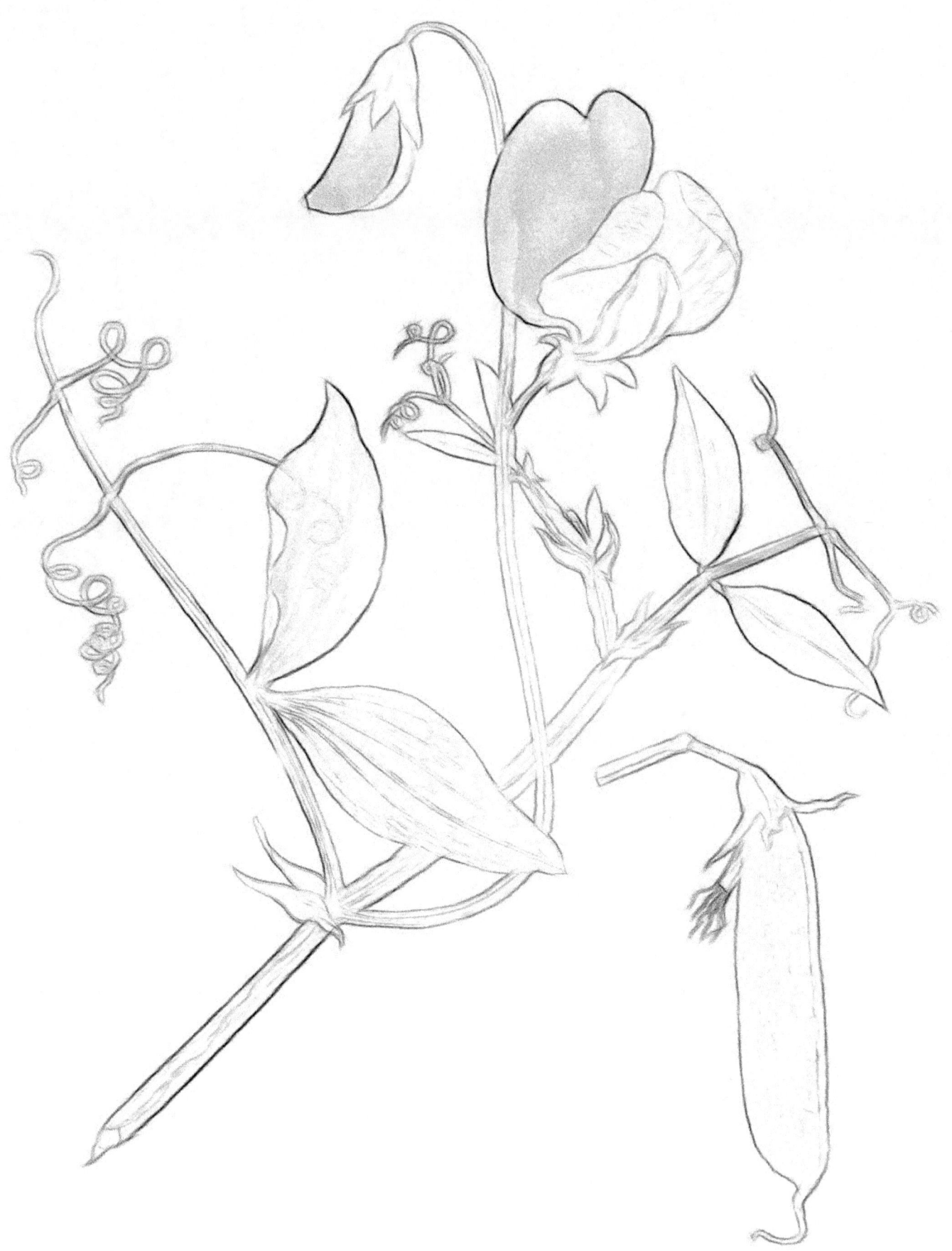

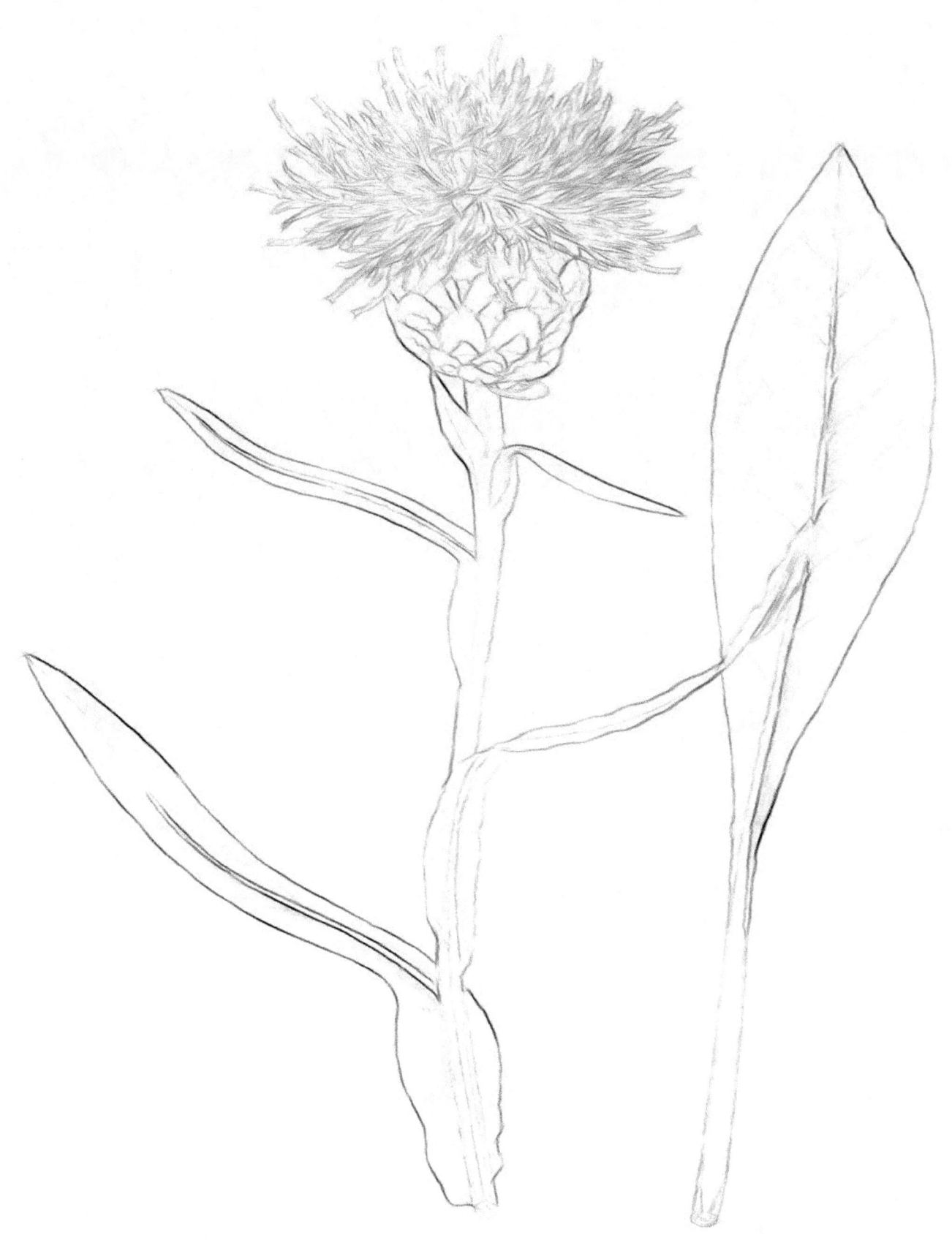

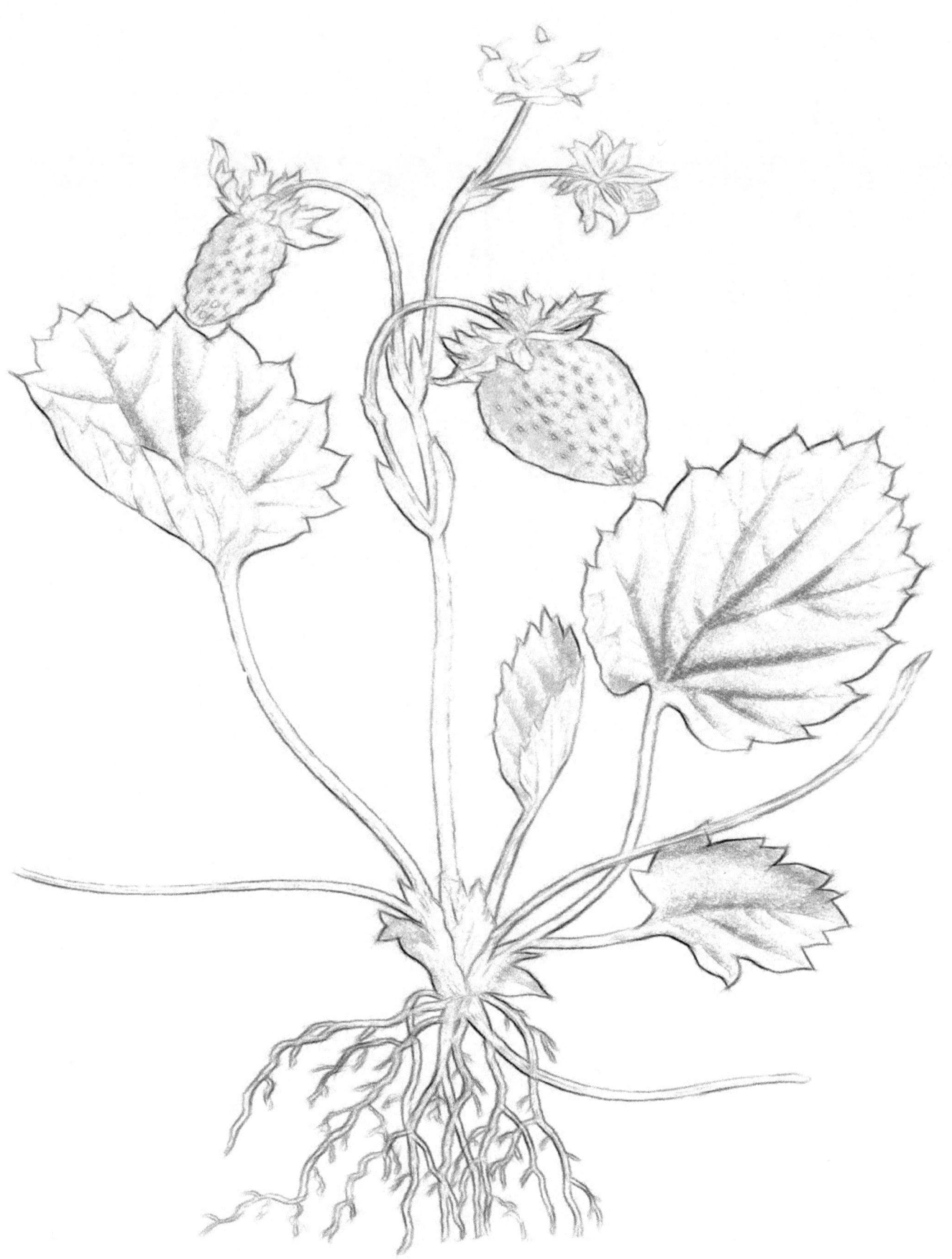

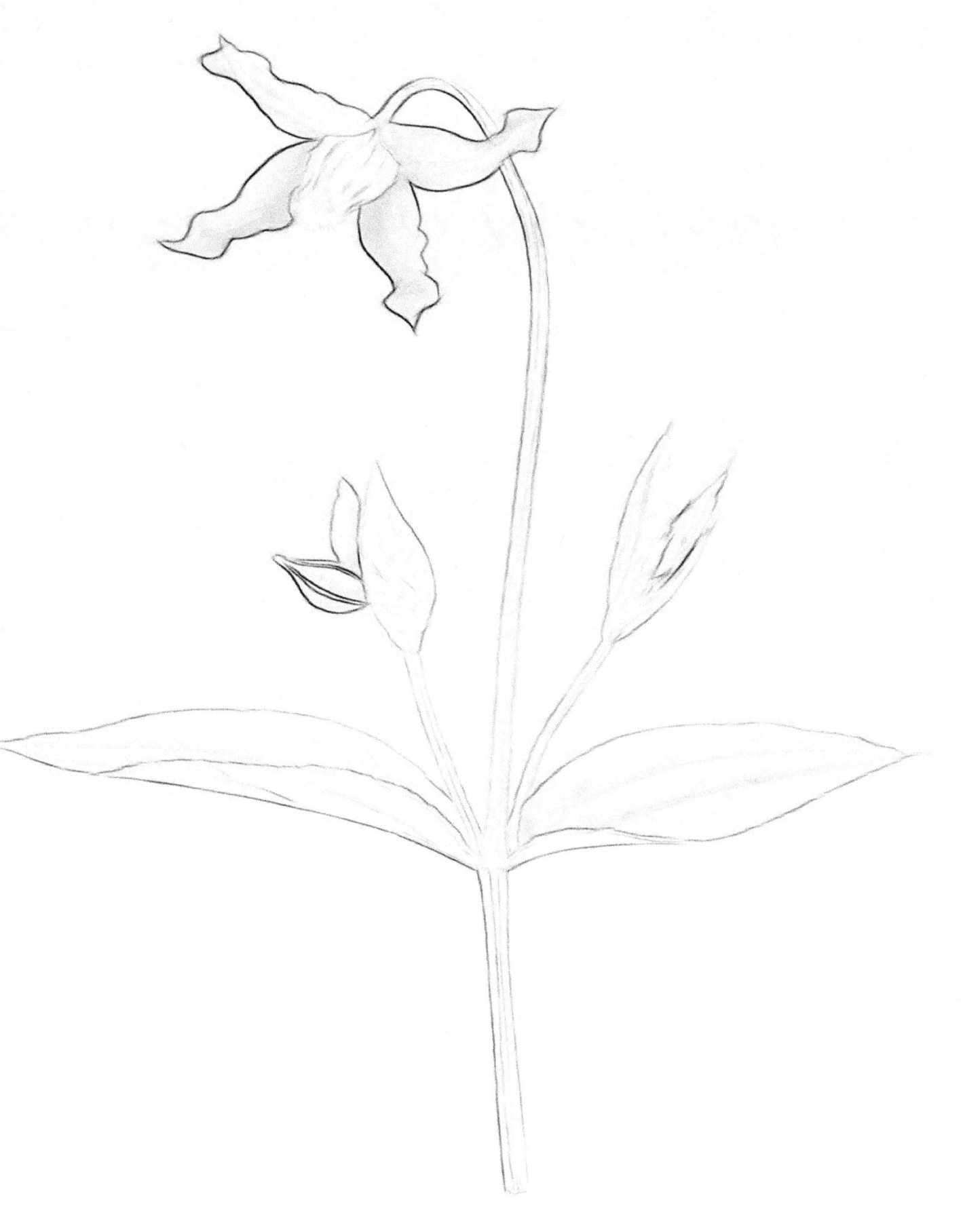

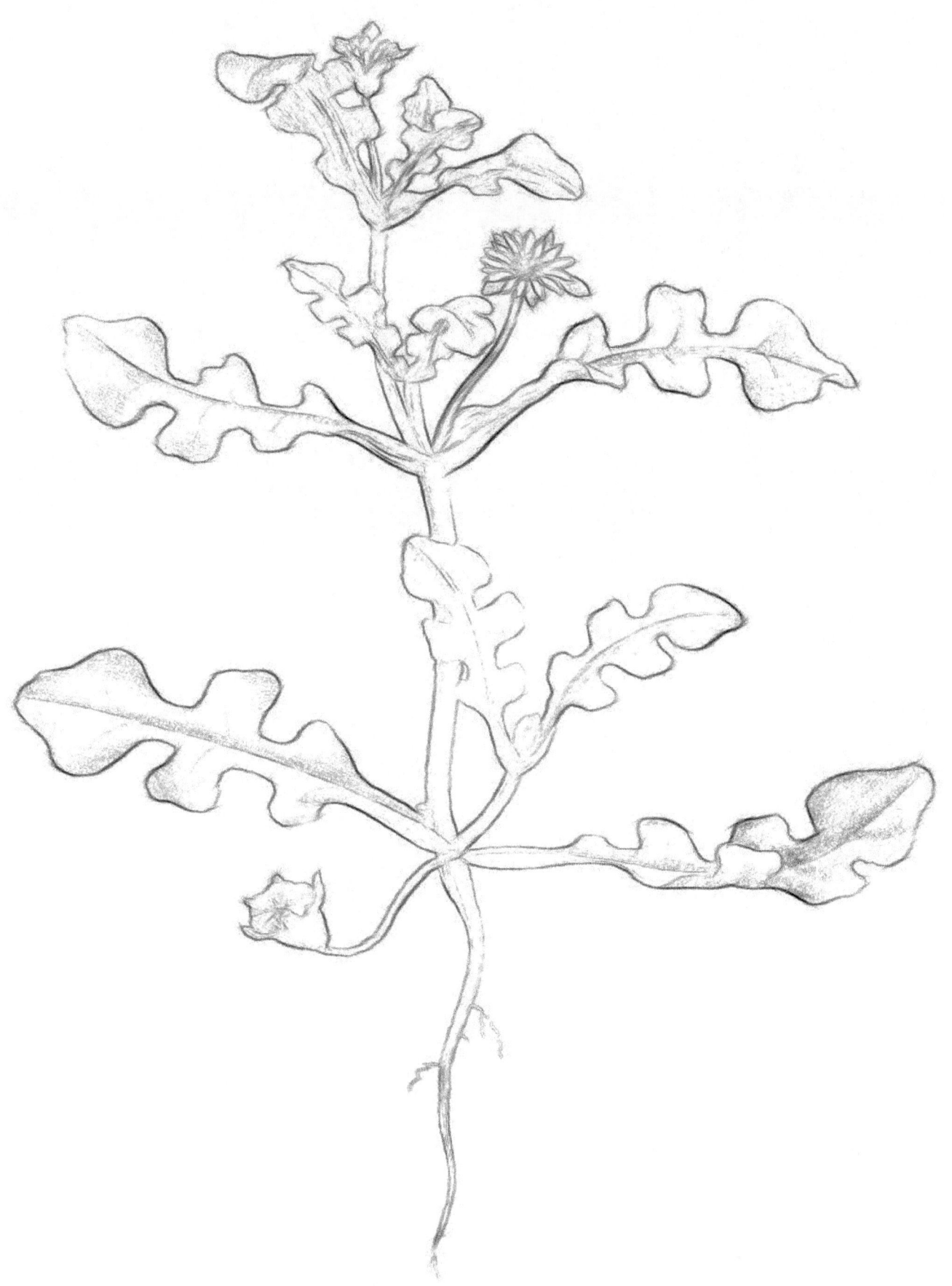

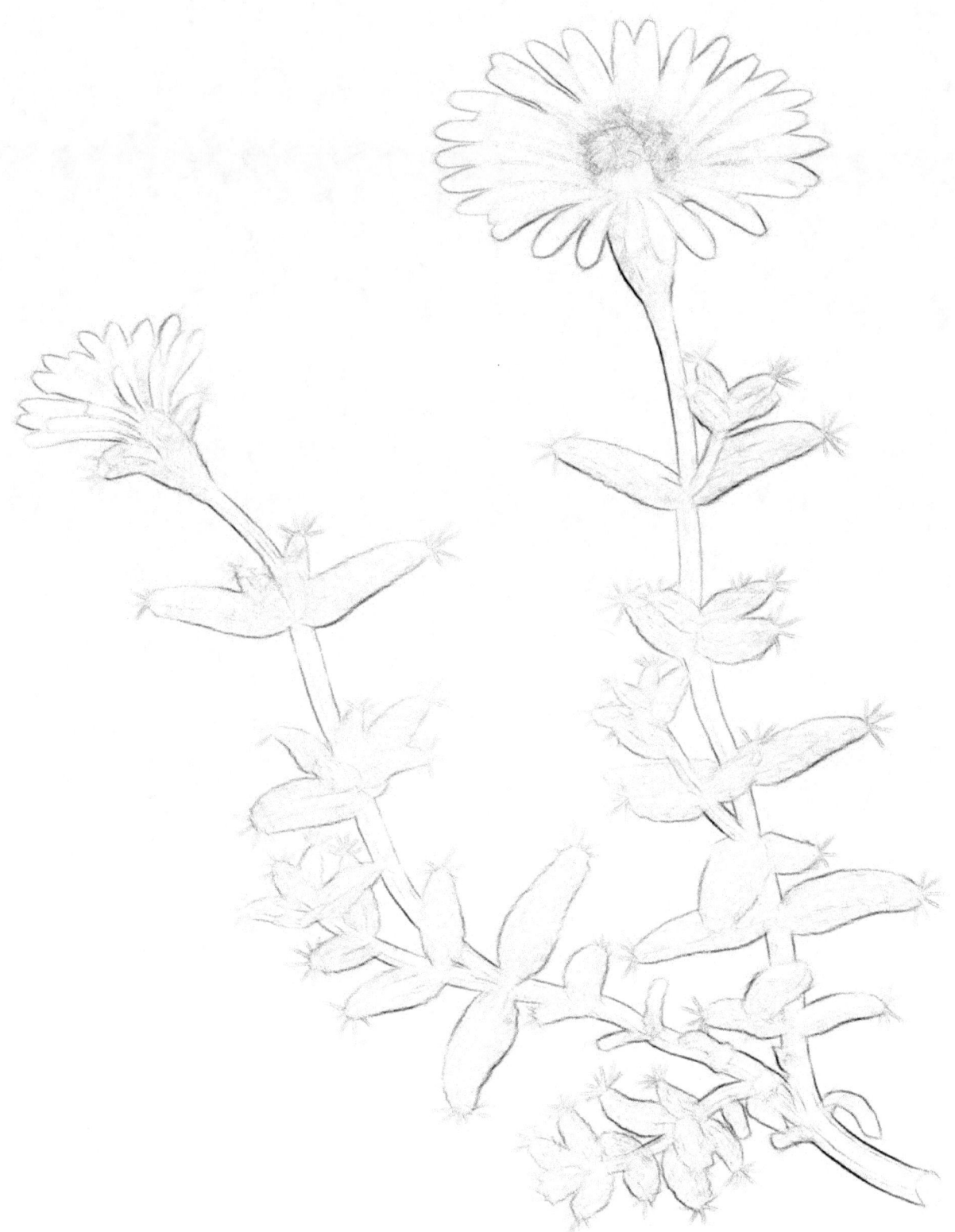

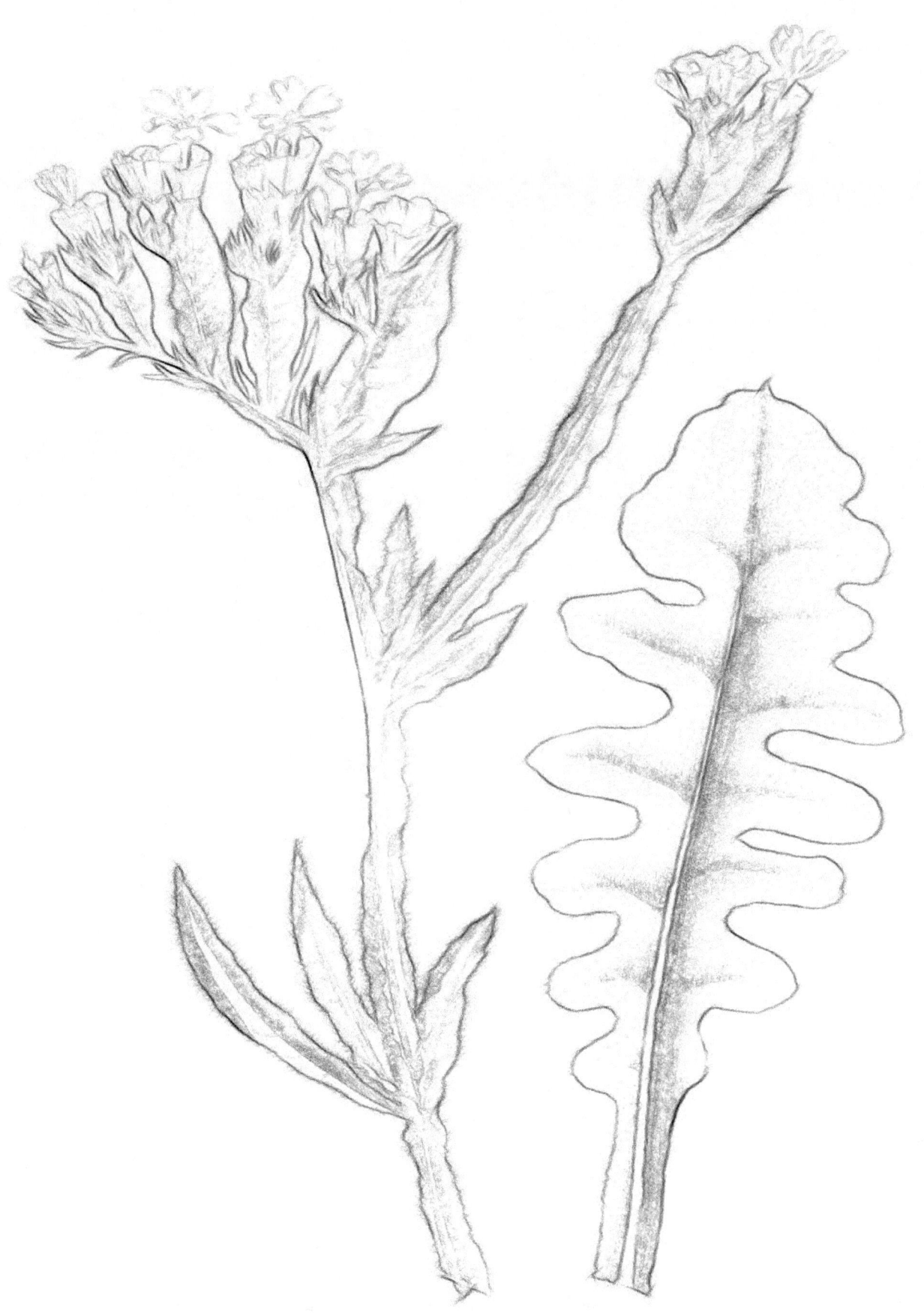

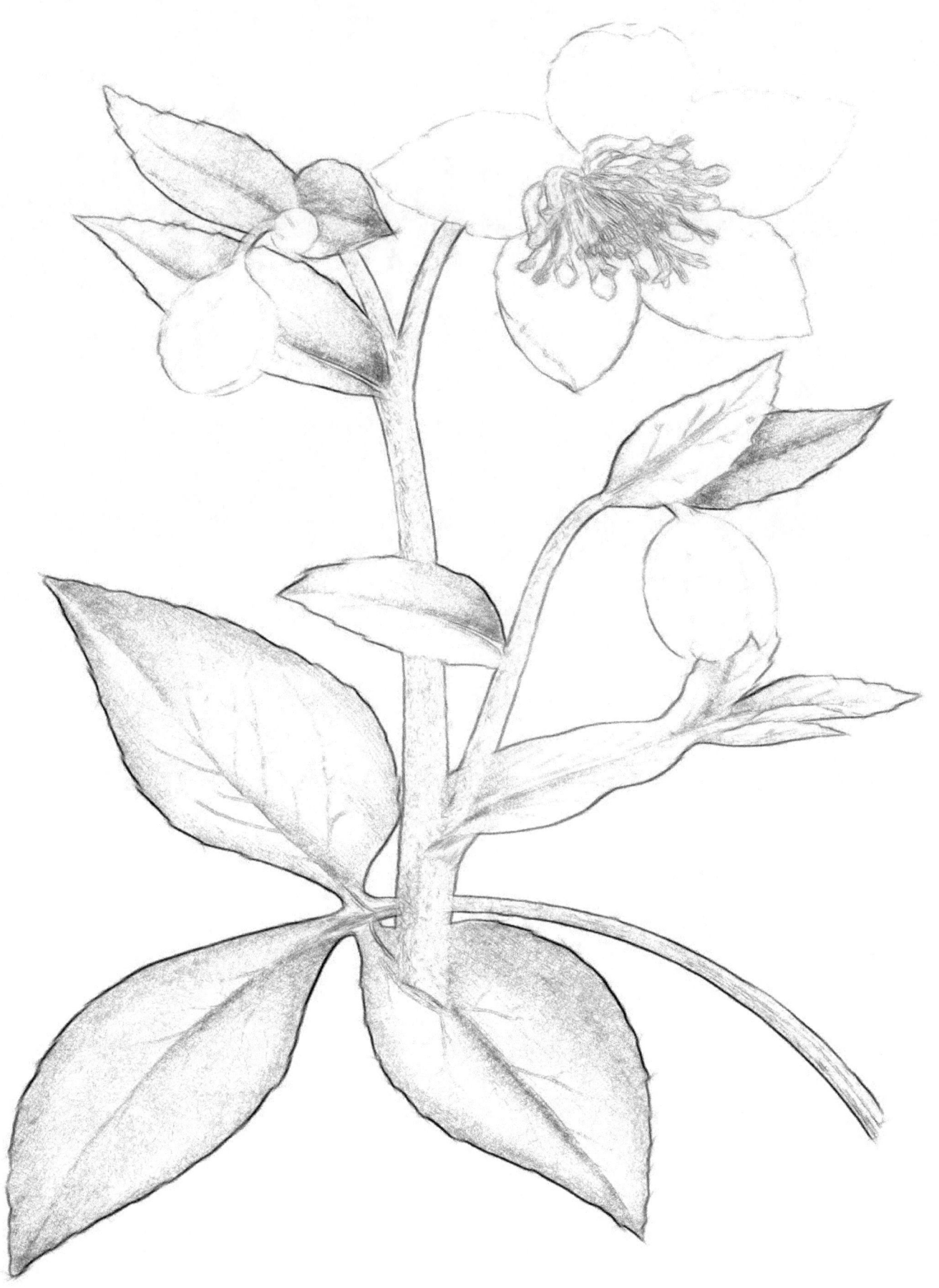

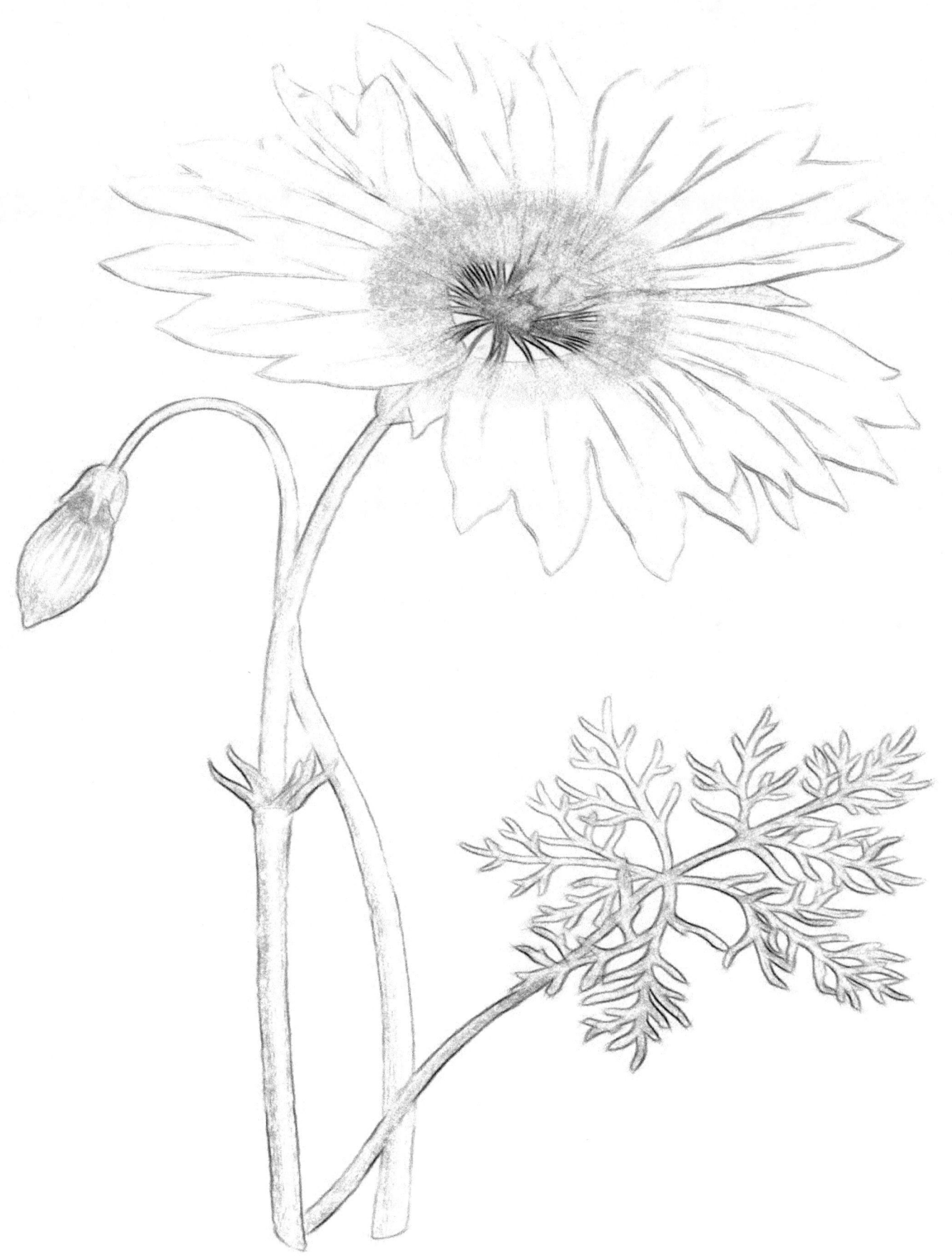

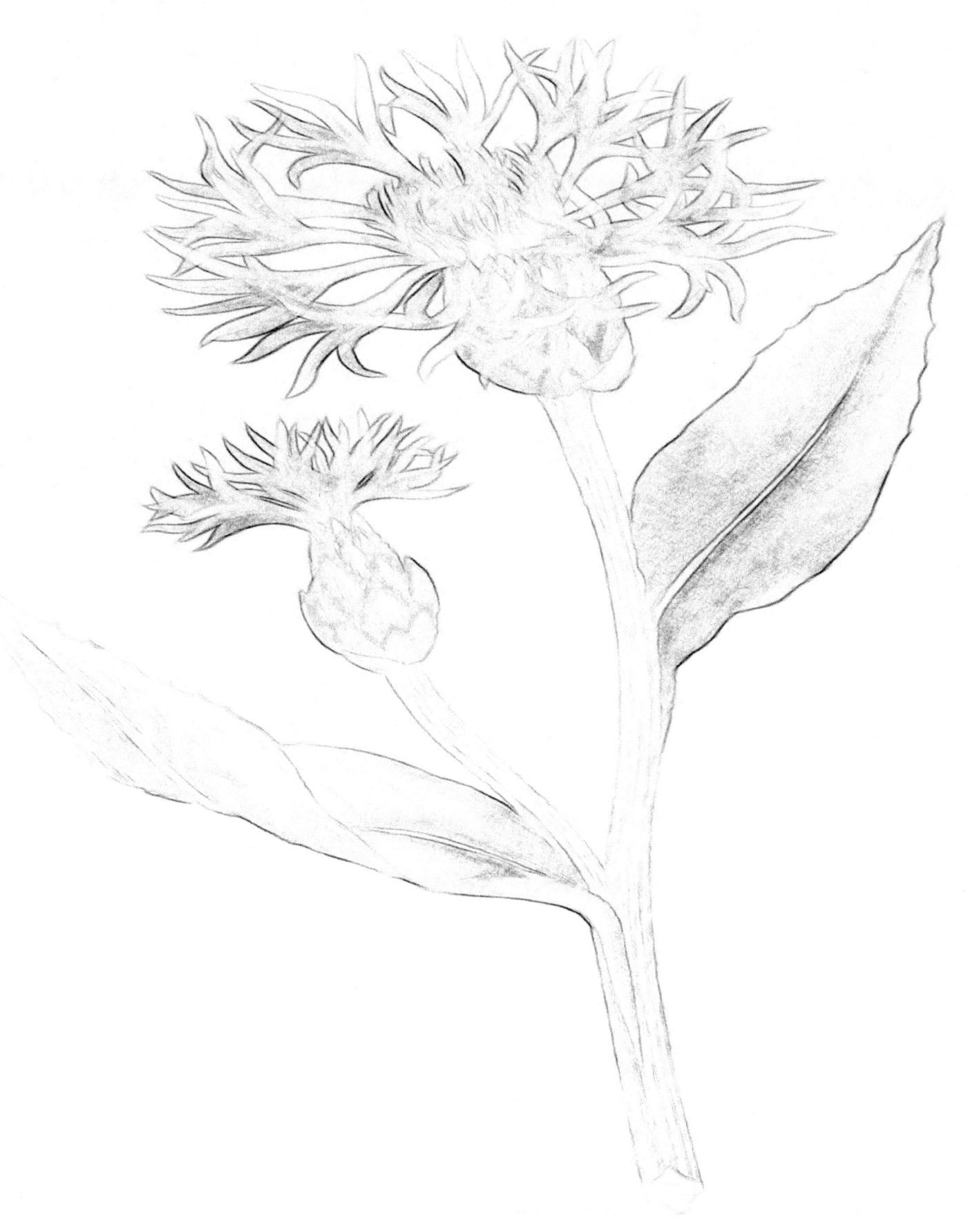

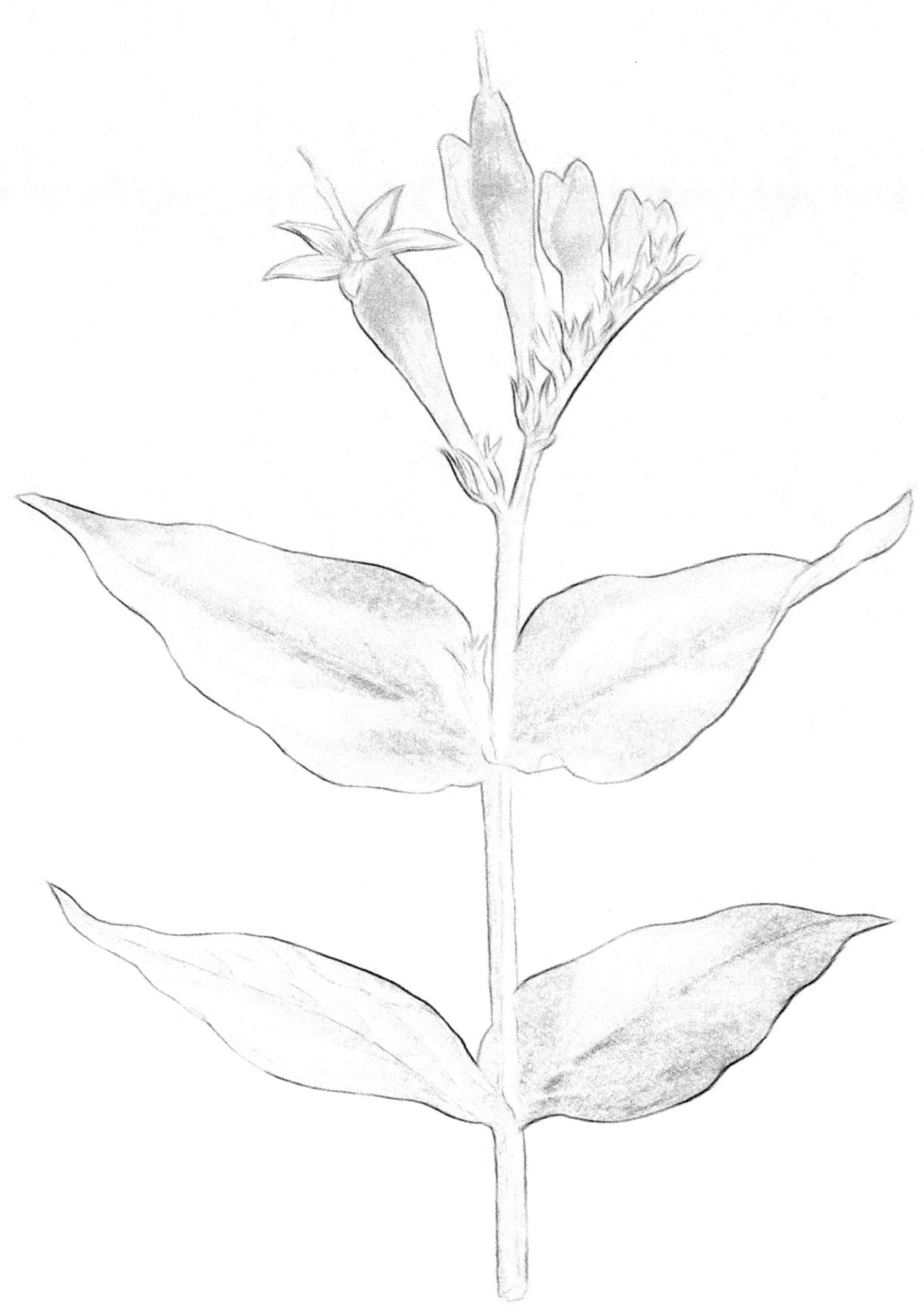

www.ingramcontent.com/pod-product-compliance
Lightning Source LLC
Chambersburg PA
CBHW080613180526
45168CB00007B/2898